Charles H. Hall

The Dutch and the Iroquois

Charles H. Hall

The Dutch and the Iroquois

ISBN/EAN: 9783337300937

Printed in Europe, USA, Canada, Australia, Japan

Cover: Foto ©Andreas Hilbeck / pixelio.de

More available books at **www.hansebooks.com**

THE DUTCH AND
THE IROQUOIS.

SUGGESTIONS AS TO
THE IMPORTANCE OF THEIR FRIENDSHIP
IN THE GREAT STRUGGLE OF THE EIGHTEENTH CENTURY
FOR THE POSSESSION OF THIS
CONTINENT.

BEING A PAPER READ BEFORE

THE LONG ISLAND HISTORICAL SOCIETY,

FEBRUARY 21, 1882.

BY THE

REV. CHARLES H. HALL, D. D.

—✤—

NEW-YORK:

PRINTED BY FRANCIS HART & COMPANY.

1882.

*T*HIS *paper follows so closely the line of thought contained in the Preface to the thirteenth volume of "Documents relating to the History of the State of New York," by Hon. Joseph B. Carr, Secretary of State, that I should cheerfully present it as the development of his thoughts, were it not true that it is an entirely independent testimony to the same. At the close of an evening, December 27, 1881, the Historical Society having listened to a paper from the Rev. Charles W. Baird, D. D., of Rye, N. Y., on "The Walloon and Huguenot Settlements of New Amsterdam," I ventured, in moving a vote of thanks to the reverend speaker, to offer the propositions herein contained, as a challenge to some descendant of the Dutch to do his ancestors justice, by substantiating them from the records of the colony. In putting my motion, the President of the Society, the Rev. Dr. Storrs, added to it a rider, that I should be requested by the Society to undertake the work. After the meeting had dissolved, the Librarian, Mr. George Hannah, informed me of the recent issue of the thirteenth volume of the*

Historical Documents, which I had not seen, and which he said would be found to confirm my expressed opinions. They do it in the main so completely that I am compelled to accept the appearance of plagiarism.

On the whole, I determined to adhere to the propositions as I made them, as the result of my own reading, and trusting to the kindly interpretation of my motives, to leave them as they really were, the independent testimony of a second witness to what I must consider one of the most remarkable facts in the history of our country, honorable to the original Dutch Colonists, and most beneficial to their successors.

The paper has been prepared under the pressure of professional duties and distractions, and is at best nothing more than suggestions as to what should be done more thoroughly by some one who has more time and ability to do full justice to the subject. It is committed to print in the hope that it may carry out my original thought of challenging some scholarly Dutchman to develop the honorable record of his ancestry. .

THE DUTCH AND THE IROQUOIS.

Mr. President, and Members of the
Long Island Historical Society:

THE propositions which I ventured to make to
you in December, and which I now offer to
develop and submit to your decision, whether they
have any substantial foundation in our colonial records, were mainly these :

First. That there was a manifest Providence in
the fact that the Dutch, rather than the English, first
came into possession of the valleys of the Hudson
and Mohawk rivers, and thus into friendly relations
with the great Amphictyonic League of the Iroquois,
originally known as the Five Nations, and later,
after their absorption by conquest of the Tuscaroras,
as the Six Nations ; that they gained their lasting
friendship and bound them by a series of treaties, to
which the English afterward succeeded, and which
were maintained without a break, until an epoch of
most remarkable interest, which, for the purposes of
this paper, I shall fix near the middle of the eighteenth century, at the fall of Quebec (1759).

Second. That after the discovery of the Mississippi River by Marquette and Joliet, in 1673, and
the completion of that discovery by La Salle, in
1682, the magnificent plan was conceived by the
ruling powers of France—first by Colbert, the financial minister of Louis XIV., who succeeded Cardinal
Mazarin, and was then and afterward pursued with
inflexible purpose and unvarying promise of success,
to confine the English and Protestant race to the
narrow region lying east of the Alleghanies.

In process of time it became known to the French
that the Iroquois held the key of the position, and
their friendship, conversion, conquest, or destruction
became of the last importance to the success of this
plan. All efforts in either direction failed, contrary
to the usual experience of the French with other
tribes, and failed because of the influences traceable
to the original impressions made by the policy of the
Dutch settlers, and bequeathed by them to the English in succession. So far as human eyes can see, it
was largely due to this fact that the vast regions
lying west of the mountain ranges, before-mentioned,
were not finally possessed and fully Latinized by the
French nation. Singularly enough, after the fall of
Quebec and the disastrous ending of this scheme,
the Iroquois willingly sought the friendship and in
numbers accepted the religion of the Catholic Church,
and many of them settled on the northern side of the
lakes and the River St. Lawrence.

Third. A subordinate proposition was submitted,
that the call of William Pitt to the head of affairs in

England, for a very brief period, was an important element in the final result. He gave unity and directness to the weak and distracted counsels, both at home and in the colonies, at the critical moment. He imparted vigor to the final campaigns, unlike all those which preceded, which drove the French and Indians from Fort Duquesne and from Fort Frontenac, and, with the regular movement of a drama, at last compelled Montcalm to account for the massacre of Fort William Henry on the plains of Abraham. But it ought never to be forgotten that the rock on which the scheme of Colbert and his successors, which would have changed the destinies of the world, was wrecked, was the inveterate hatred of the Six Nations to the French, or, in other words, their friendship originally secured by the few humble Dutch colonists of Fort Orange, where the city of Albany now stands.

In developing such a series of propositions, extending from 1609, or say 1621, until the middle of the succeeding century (1759), and rich in so many side-issues, you perceive that one must and can follow only a single thread of history, and establish only certain pregnant facts between very narrow limits.

First of all, then, by way of preface, allow me to say a few words on what is meant by *"a manifest Providence."* I do not intend to draw on your faith in the supernatural or the miraculous. I include in the word a vast field of that human ignorance where men are seeking only their own private ends, and aiming only at objects in the limits of their narrow horizon, while they are really working out some mighty order of destiny which lies far outside of their vision. I include all that we call accidents, "that work together for good," that come unforeseen or seemingly disappointing. to the actors in them, whose importance is unfelt at the time, whose immediate results are feebly recognized, and whose ultimate consequences are beyond the calculations of the wisest statesmen.

All these may be only the evolutions of an insensible cellule. They may be the accidents of unthinking Fate. They may be, as well, the movements of a vast Mind.

Let me ask you, first of all, to consider the geographical features of the continent, which enter into the subject. Look with the mind's eye upon the topography of the United States, only remembering that it was altogether unknown to the early colonists. Passing up the River St. Lawrence, and through Lake Ontario, and by the Niagara into the next lake, you reach the port of Erie, first known as Presque Isle, a distance of about nine hundred miles from the sea. Threading the shallow stream of Muddy Creek, and making a portage of a half-dozen miles, you can launch a canoe on the head-waters of the French Creek, a tributary of the Alleghany River, and float on its rapid current some two hundred and eighty-five miles to the city of Pittsburg. From thence to the Gulf of Mexico, by way of the Ohio River, the distance is two thousand and twenty-eight miles. You have now in mind the greatest inland waterway on the globe—over thirty-five hundred miles in length—in these two vast basins. They are still the subjects of wildest speculation as to their future populations, their prospective wealth, and political importance. The River St. Lawrence, draining waters which have entered the western end of Lake Superior through the *dalles* of the St. Louis River, twelve hundred and fifty miles west of Kingston, runs seven hundred and fifty miles eastwardly to its terminal point at Cape Chatte—in all, two thousand miles. It drains a water-shed of four hundred thousand square miles. Beginning from its prime sources in the western prairies and hackmatack swamps of Minnesota, it was computed by Darby, before the discovery of the great African lakes, to contain "more than half the fresh water on the globe." A vessel of five hundred tons can, to-day, load at Duluth, some two thousand miles from the Atlantic, and "break bulk" in any port in the world.*

Again, one can hardly mention the name of the *Miche-sepe*, the Father of Waters, without a spasm of the imagination such as our poet, Drake, must have felt when he seemed to see "Freedom from her mountain height," wherever that may have been, in a rampant humor "tearing the azure robe of night," and setting "the stars of glory" in her flag of "manifest destiny." It is—the Nile, possibly, excepted—the longest river in the world, and

* There are two other natural connections between these great basins, farther west, by which the French traveled to discover the great river—namely, the one by Chicago and by the Illinois River, and the other through Green Bay, by the Fox and Wisconsin rivers. But the route I have indicated above was the one which they at last endeavored to occupy and hold for the purpose of securing the command of this continent.

drains a region almost equal to the continent of Europe. From the cool trout-lakes of Upper Minnesota it is about two thousand nine hundred and eighty-six miles long, and, by the Missouri branch, four thousand five hundred and six miles, and receives the waters of fifteen hundred tributaries. It drains an area of one million two hundred and fifty-four thousand square miles. It bears an annual tribute to its delta, in sediment, of a square mile of earth two hundred and forty-one feet in thickness. Reckoning all its branches, it forms a natural waterway of fifteen thousand miles. De Soto, the Spaniard, in search of an El Dorado, was the first white who, in 1541, stood on its banks somewhere up the stream, and found his grave in its bosom. The story of Père Marquette and the trader Joliet, in 1673, descending its current to some point within three days' journey of its mouth, reads now like a romance. It fired alike the imagination of the Chevalier de la Salle, at Fort Frontenac; of Talon, the Intendant of Canada, at Quebec; and of Colbert, at Paris. The former, like Themistocles at the victories of Miltiades, could not rest till he had reached its mouth and determined its position—whether in the Gulf of California, or of Mexico, or in the Atlantic Ocean.

We may pause for a moment to glance at the region which France sold to the United States in 1803, for fifteen million dollars, which was a mere fragment and chattel mortgage of the vast territory, to which she once aspired and very nearly secured. That fragment sold to us was "all the region west of the Mississippi not occupied by Spain, reaching north to the British possessions," being the States of Louisiana, Arkansas, Kansas, Iowa, Minnesota, Missouri, Nebraska, Oregon, the Indian Territory, Colorado, Dakota, Montana, and Washington Territory. Fancy what New France might have been, had their plan of empire succeeded. I ask you again to remember now, that in 1609, when Champlain joined a war-party of Algonquins at Hochelaga, the Island of Montreal, these vast regions were entirely unknown. Europeans looked west from the lip of the sea, on interminable forests, ignorant of their contents, creeping along the shores, or penetrating the bays, in hopes that some channel might lead them at once to the spice islands of golden Cathay. The principal object of the gay and gallant chevalier in joining the Algonquins was the discovery of the wilderness above Montreal. The numbers of the party were increased by a chance meeting with some Hurons, and together they reached, on a bright May morning, the leafy shores of the lake which bears his name. They were suddenly attacked by a band of Mohawks, the terror then of all the tribes. One of those accidents on which the imagination is apt to linger occurred there. On the advancing warriors, who had been hitherto invincible, Champlain discharged his arquebuse with deadly effect. Terrified at this novel mode of slaughter, they fled in confusion, and told to their castles the story of a new race of pale faces, who carried the lightning in their hands, and smote their enemies from a distance with the noise of thunder. It may be doubted if the echo of that morning fire of an arquebuse ever ceased to vibrate on the nerve of Mohawk memory. It was about the only result of the expedition.

The same year, not without hope that he might be looking into the channel which would lead to India, Hendrick Hudson entered the Bay of Manathe, or Manhattan, and groped up the river as far as the falls at Cohoes. He returned home to tell the merchants of England and Holland of the great river that bears his name. Nineteen years afterward the Pilgrims left Leyden, intending to make a settlement on this river of Hudson, but were treacherously landed on Massachusetts Bay. In 1629 Sir David Kirke took Quebec from Champlain. It was restored to the French three years afterward, 1632, ninety-seven years after Jacques Cartier had reached it and found an Indian village there; and had been visited by Donnacona, the *Agonhanna*, or King of Canada. A century had passed, and it was little more than an Indian village still, with a French trader wandering thither now and then, little dreaming of the fierce contest which should yet be fought out for an empire, on its far-famed summit.

May I ask you here to notice another geographical feature which enters into the great struggle which was then to come? It is the subordinate water-way, with its short portage at Fort Edward, which connects the River St. Lawrence with New York Bay. A canoe starting from Quebec can reach with little difficulty the southern end of Lake Champlain, or of Lake George. Thence, by a portage of a few miles to Glen's Falls, or Fort Edward, it may be launched on the swift current of the Hudson River and landed at Manhattan Island. You will remember the important part which this natural passage played so late as the Revolution of 1776, when first General Burgoyne and Sir Henry Clinton attempted to gain possession of it, and thus to dissever the colonies, that they might conquer them in detail. Afterward Major André lost his life and Arnold his honor, by a second attempt to gain by craft what they had failed to secure by force. The dangers to the Dutch and English colonists from this source were early appreciated by all parties, and the French once tried to take possession of it by a land force transported over the lakes coöperating with a naval attack on New York. It was, too, over this water-way that the marauding parties of French and Indians often journeyed, whose night-howls announced massacre and captivity to the terrified villagers of the Connecticut and Mohawk valleys.

These, then, are the geographical features which enter into my propositions, and will help to explain the course of our national history. The elevated plateau which extends from the Green Mountains south to the Kaatskills, and west across the State to Lake Erie, and southward again to the Pennsylvania line, sheds its waters into the Atlantic at Sandy Hook, into the Northern Ocean by the St. Lawrence, and into the Gulf of Mexico by the Alleghany, the Ohio, and the Mississippi rivers. During the period of colonial history when the canoe and the batteaux were the only means of inland conveyance, and the arquebuse and patereros were the chief weapons ot offensive warfare, this region was the key of the continent. When Joliet revealed to France the true course of the Mississippi, it became the natural policy of the French Government to gain possession of it, and to keep the English from it. If they had succeeded—and they did nearly succeed—in gaining the alliance of the tribes living upon that plateau ; if their agents, everywhere else possessed of fascinations to charm the savage mind by their unparalleled heroism, by their unequaled daring as traders and hunters, or as discoverers and chivalrous soldiers ; by appeals to Indian vanity and self-interest, and no less by exciting their respect and fear, in that they saw all other tribes coming willingly under the influence of the French, and they in danger of being hemmed in on the north and west by powerful enemies, and left to the feeble support of timid and half-hearted allies; if they could have gained this one object of their ambition, it is little to say, that, so far as we can see, this continent would now be under the power and religious teaching of the Latin races.

It will be found that the Five Nations were the rock of resistance to oppose and defeat these plans. The Iroquois are always recognized by the French in this light. They resisted for a century and a half the flatteries and menaces of the French, and kept unexampled faith with the Dutch and English to the end of the contest.

It is, therefore, of prime interest to us to know something of the character and motives of these savages, to whom we owe so much. They are by no means a lovely set. They are, in some things, a horrible race. None the less they are the happiest of accidents in our past history. It gives me satisfaction here to corroborate my statements by the authority of the last volume of the Documents relating to the colonial history of this State. It is there stated that the Five Nations "had possession of the very key to this continent, and they had been masters of a large portion of it, and ruled the tribes from Maine to the Mississippi, and as far south as Georgia." The same industrious compiler agrees with me, "that we can only congratulate ourselves, as citizens of the State of New York, that the first white men with whom the Indians of this section of the American continent had to deal were the upright and sturdy, even if slow and phlegmatic, Dutch.'* Other causes coöperated with this fortunate circumstance, which serve to explain it.

The general name by which the quarter of a million or less of American aborigines were known in the seventeenth century was "the Algonquins." It seems to have been the name of a particular tribe, which lived upon the Ottawa River, who were enemies to the Iroquois. It was the luck of the French to come first upon them and other such enemies of the Five Nations, and to rouse against themselves the active hatred of the latter. Champlain, as I have said, in 1609, eager for discovery, came into hostile collision with the Mohawks, and taught them the terrible power of fire-arms, and no less the inappeasable detestation of his race. Again, in 1615, he joined their ancient enemies, the Hurons, in an

---

* Doct. of Col. Hist., Vol. XIII., p. v.

expedition against one of their towns in the interior of this State. Therefore, in 1632, when that nation recovered Canada, and began the continuous history of "New France," they found the Five Nations predominant, and fiercely determined in hostility to them. Seventeen years before—that is, in 1615—these tribes had already made a firm treaty with the Dutch at Fort Orange, had learned from them the use of fire-arms, and had invaded Canada with their old success. They at once shut off the French from Lake Ontario, and compelled them to pursue their objects of settlement, by means of the Hurons, around Georgian Bay. For a long period no priest or trapper was bold enough to attempt the passage of the St. Lawrence, or to be seen on Lake Ontario; and even, in tracking the cold Ottawa, they were often waylaid and murdered by these wakeful foes.

These Iroquois, as the French called them, or Maguas,— that is, Bears, as they were known to the Dutch and the Algonquins,— were found to consist of five separate nations, which were bound together by an ancient league, which appears as the first rude step, and the only one known to the aborigines, of an incipient civilization. They were called, among themselves, "Maguas," "Oneidas," "Onondagas," "Cayugas," and "Senecas." The first tribe dwelt in the Hudson and Mohawk valleys, and the others along the lakes which bear their names.

This league is called by Colden, who compiled his facts as early as 1727, though his history appeared in 1747, "immemorial," and it gave them the common name of "Konoshioni," the "Cabin-makers," or "People of the long house"! This long house, metaphorically, reached from the river to the shore of Lake Erie. The eastern door of it was the Maguas. The council-fire was on the shores of Lake Onondaga, where always an Onondaga chief, who was known as the "Atotarho," presided and had charge of the sacred fire. Each tribe was subdivided into three clans or sections, and each clan was a separate and independent democracy in itself, distinguished by its "totem," or badge, of the wolf, the bear, and the tortoise. They proudly called themselves the "Ongue-honwe"—the men surpassing all others. As their league-name implies, they had advanced far enough in civilization to build castles,— rude structures enough, but very effective fortresses for all the warfare which was then known among them. These castles were in some cases roomy habitations, or, again, groups of huts, surrounded by a strong palisade and trench.

What they had of history points us to some period of the sixteenth century, when they were living on the banks of the St. Lawrence, around the island of Montreal. They were then corn-planters. The Algonquins were hunters living at some distance from them to the north. They supplied each other's wants by a sort of rude commerce, until the proud hunting tribes broke out into war against them, overcame them, and steadily pursued them across the river and the lakes to the center of this State. There for a time they continually wasted away, until at last they learned from bitter experience the wisdom of union. They put aside their meaner quarrels with each other, and

2

entered into the league of the "Konoshioni," or castle-
builders. From that time they began to make head
against their foes. They rose by constant success to
a superior condition, and carried their "totems" in terror over half the continent. A single Magua brave
has been known, from mere wantonness, to enter a
town of the hostile Abenakis, or Eastern Indians, and
play for an hour the part of Achilles among the
Myrmidons. The poetry of Street is hardly exag-
gerated, in which he describes the prowess of these
savages, which gave them some right to call themselves the "Ongue-honwe," the Anaxanders, the
Anakims of this Western' world.

> " The fierce Adirondacks had fled from their wrath,
>   The Hurons been swept from their merciless path ;
>   Around the Ottawas like leaves had been strown,
>   And the Lake of the Eries struck silent and lone.
>   The Lenape, lords once of valley and hill,
>   Made women, bent low at the conqueror's will.
>   By the far Mississippi the Illini shrank,
>   When the trail of the Tortoise was seen on the bank ;
>   On the hills of New England the Pequod turned pale,
>   When the howl of the Wolf swelled at night on the gale,
>   And the Cherokee shook in his green smiling bowers,
>   When the foot of the Bear stamped his carpet of flowers."

"Their invincible arms," says Brodhead, "humbled
every native foe, and their national pride grew with
every conquest." *

My first proposition is, that it was well for us that
the Dutch came first into contact with these people,
and not the English nor the French. It is not worth

---

* Quoted by Brodhead, Hist. St. of N. Y., First Period, p. 87.

your while either to praise or abuse them. Certain facts stand out unquestioned, and will partly explain their conduct. They were superior to all other tribes, and they ought to be, compared with them; and all together should be compared,— or contrasted, if you will,—not with ourselves, but with the men of earlier and ruder civilizations,—with Autochthones of European peninsulas, Druids of German or British woods, or with the savage tribes of other continents. The question is not what we can sentimentally say of them as "Stoics of the woods, the men without a tear," but just how it came to pass that they were able and ready to make an abiding compact— "an iron chain," as they called it—with such civilized men as they found at Fort Orange in 1615, and to observe that compact with undisturbed probity during a century pregnant with important issues.

They were splendid animals in their physique, when the white men first fell in with them—animals at the head of our Western organisms. They had not idealized the powers of savage nature about them into dreamy idolatries. Their language proves that they had no habit of reflection or faculty of analysis. They were content to hold and cherish—on a plane which is probably inconceivable to us—a profound sympathy with the most savage things in nature. There was in them a measureless stupidity of imagination as to things abstract. Their own perfect physical organisms were closely in sympathy with the wild denizens of the forest. They honored the wolf, whose totem was their mark of aristocracy, their Order of the Garter, the oriflamme of their chivalry, the catechism of their moral training, the gaunt hero of their imaginations. They had by heredity an infinite savagery, before which we weaker invalids shrink back appalled. We have violently reached some recesses of crime — they sounded all with a masterful genius. Who like the wolf to them, whose howlings in the thicket, terrific to civilized men, were to them, by the training of generations, the music of religious love? Like him, they lived on what the forest supplied. They could steal over the withered leaves on their deadly trail as silently as he, as hungry for blood, as insatiable and remorseless, as terrible in their final spring, as daring at last to the bitter end, when all arts failed, as grim and untamable in death. They tuned their war-whoop to his howl, and the only music which ever resounded through their settlements, whether in war song or funeral lament, was a wail as harsh and rude as his. They emulated his cunning, and what we should call his treachery. It was no shame—it was glory to their young warriors—to model their honor by this fiercest and most dangerous animal of their forests. We call it the hungry wolf. The lynx is keener of vision, the panther larger, but each can be appeased or turned aside. It was a sense to them of the hungry wolf, that identified him with them, as the ideal sublime. Untiring, insatiable, moved by a mystical scent from afar, turning aside for no obstacle, knowing no pause or fatigue, insensible to cold or heat, he had in his make-up no suggestion of any weakness of mercy or honor to check his one fierce craving for blood.

Or, next, they chose the "Magua," the Bear, as the god of their warlike idolatry. Dark, mysterious, cowardly as we know him, given to the meanest panics and most ignominious victories over defenseless victims, he was no coward to them. He suggested no ignominy who could prowl around their paths unseen, and, when brought to bay, would silently give the deadly hug, but would yield no sign at the keen knife in his ribs, but die in fierce embrace, with immense rage, and without a sign of remorse or fear.

Again, they found in the tortoise a poem of silent hate, an animal Odyssey of cunning. We may call it sneaking and stupid, a poor reptile, whose insignificance seems to be his highest praise ; but we have little right to offer our critical judgment for their condemnation in these matters, till we recall on the one side our own historical antecedents, which have created our national symbols of thought, having barely escaped the rattlesnake on our flag, in favor of the eagle—greediest, and, in some regards, the vilest of birds; or, on the other side, until we realize in some degree what must have been the mental condition of men who knew nothing beyond ceaseless internecine warfare ; men whose imaginations held no gentler or better thoughts than wolves, bears, and reptiles had in common with them. Singularly enough, those tribes had a code of honor with the rattlesnake, and are said to keep to it still. If he strikes at them after rattling his dread defiance, they pass on and leave him uninjured. They respect him. But, if he strikes without it, they hunt him to the death.

These were the human animals of whom I speak. There was in them an educated capacity of infinite hate. The women of the tribes appear to have surpassed the men in fidelity to their ferocious creed. They were always the principal actors in the doleful records of tortures to captives. Of course, I am not admiring this quality in them; but I do respect consistency, even in the Devil. Hate was their religion. The women were their sublime hierophants. They are said to be always more religious than men. These were. They taught it to their children. There is always a down-look—there is to-day—in the savage, a moral flat-headedness, melancholic, atrabilious, horrible. Let us grant them at least the one alleviation of consistency.

Just here I cannot resist the temptation to turn aside for a word to my imaginative friends, who claim to find sermons in stones, and books in running brooks—to the disparagement of Bibles, creeds, and churches. They tell us of Bryant, who discovered on these same uplands how "the groves were God's first temples," where

> "An invisible Breath in all their green tops bowed
> Man's spirit with the thought of boundless power
> And inaccessible majesty. And why
> Should we, in the world's riper years, neglect
> God's ancient sanctuaries, and adore
> Only among the crowd and under roofs
> That our own frail hands have raised?"

Why, indeed! Mark, if you please, that the poet states it as an historical fact that the original races learned their religions by these means. There has been a time with me, in youth, on a June day, when

> "All the green leaves over me,
> Clapped their little hands in glee,
> With one continuous sound"—

that I have accepted, not his poetical charm,—for that we all feel,—but his historical accuracy. Pardon my later skepticism. What Bryant found in the "calm shades" which taught him that we must "conform the order of our lives" "to the beautiful order of God's works," he had previously learned elsewhere, in temples made by humble hands; from the ages when Moses, who had had enough of lonely deserts, stretched his tent of "dyed badger-skins" to centralize a nation's worship, and thus secure its virtue; from ages when Christians built their first churches of wattles, and plastered them with clay; and from brown, unpainted New England or Dutch meeting-houses, beneath whose benign influences a merciful nation rose to majestic power here, and made the poet's wood-wanderings safe for him. I leave you to explain how it was that these Maguas failed to spell out a word of the Forest Hymn in the groves of the Empire State. It was well for us, on the whole, that the colonists did their worship mainly under cover, and in reach of their muskets, or these sylvan devotees might have disturbed the even tenor of their devotions. The Iroquois had learned a far different lesson in our forests—the lesson of hate. This hatred, by nature, by heredity, and by education, was an important element in my proposition. They first approached the Dutch with hearts full of detestation of the French. Their first wish was for fire-arms.

For ages immemorial in their simple annals, the Algonquins, Adirondacks, and Hurons had been their enemies. At a flash they were driven back before them in terror, no less in mortification. And again, these enemies had dared to invade their forests almost to the place of their league-hearth. I am not inclined to indulge the dramatic vein, but it was certainly unlucky for him that Champlain should have appeared before them as the friend of the detested and despised Hurons. The compact which the Mohawks made with the Dutch was secured partly by their sublime faculty of enduring animal hatred.

Again, the Iroquois were a cruel race. The accounts of their ingenuity in torturing their captives would sicken a tiger, if he could be made to understand it. One wonders, in reading the narrative of Father Isaac Jogues, whether the Fiend himself could have done more, if he had been present. The history of the Inquisition reads tame after it. I will not pursue the theme.*

They were vain to extreme silliness—"pleased with a rattle and tickled with a straw"—when the braggart nerve was touched. They were drunkards by predetermined viciousness. There was nothing in the animal catechism, there was nothing learned by them in wood or leaf, on lake or stream, which could give them a shadow of a dream of virtuous self-restraint. Their older chiefs begged piteously

* Doc., etc., etc., Vol. xiii., Appendix A, p. 577.

and stormed eloquently to the civilized men to keep
the "brandy kegs" away from the tribes, because no
Indian could resist temptation, and then they went
aside to indulge in debauch. In matters of family
life, virtue had no name among them. They learned
no one of the ten commandments from wolves and
bears, and did not improve on their example. To
sum up this darker side, they were pure and simple
animals, of stout health and vigor, able to endure
great hardship in the chase and upon the war-path,
when appetite and revenge were driving them, and
they were little more. But they were a little more.
They had begun to reach upward, to almost the only
thing known to the aborigines of a constitutional
government. Fierce and intractable, they were pain-
fully independent and restless of the least restraint.

Each clan, yea, every solitary cabin or castle, was
a republic. They would have no leader over them,
except as he was successful. The aged warrior who
had been for years a victor fell into disgrace, if he
was once defeated. Yet we read of one virtue in
their chiefs, which some would recommend to our
own chiefs and city fathers—they were mostly poor,
on principle. They could indulge any love of power
only by resigning all profits of the chase or spoils of
war to their followers.

Another virtue in them—I am afraid to analyze
too closely, lest it should vanish in the handling—
was some practical sense of the value and obligation
of treaties. Their original league was "immemorial."
Probably for a century it had somehow taught them
the lesson necessary to any civilization. Once they

had nearly perished by division. They had become a great power by union. Rudest in forms and curious to study, they possessed a sort of general government, which held them together for certain purposes. They met often at the council-fire at Onondaga, and discussed in some stormy manner the questions of peace and war. Intractable, they yielded submission to the decrees which issued from thence, and the totem sent abroad, like the fire-tipped cross of the Scotch Highlanders, was recognized by every tribe or solitary hunter as a call which was to be instantly obeyed. Launching their canoes on the lakes or on the head-waters of the various rivers that flowed every way from their country, they made expeditions against the Abenakis at the forks of the Kennebec, the Hurons around Georgian Bay, the Miamis, Chippeways, and Sioux of the West, and the Tuscaroras and Cherokees of the South. They did it as a nation, rather than as single tribes. At the remonstrance of the Governor of Maryland, we read of them once calling the Oneidas and Senecas to account for invasions on Southern tribes. This is a small quantum of virtue to find in a race, but it is the one virtue which was of the last importance to us. Beside their hatred of the French, we must grant them a knowledge of the advantage of treaties, and intelligence enough to account for the fact that they did make and observe them as no other Western tribes did. Colden claims for them "a bright and noble genius shining through their inheritance of darkest ignorance," and compares them, as Volney also has done, to the ancient Romans.

But it is a suspicious circumstance of this commendation, that, antedating General Sherman's remark "that a good Indian is a dead Indian," he offers as proof of this noble genius their ability to die. It were well if we could find in them more of a genius to live decently and soberly. He terms them "the fiercest and most formidable people in North America, and, at the same time, as politic and judicious as can be conceived." ·

These were the men of the Five Nations, the door of whose "great house" were the Mohawks. Knowing nothing of the importance of the spot to them and to us, the Dutch, for purposes of trade solely, came wandering up the Ca-ho-ha-ta-tea, the "river splitting the mountains," — our Hudson, — passed by the Algonquin tribes, who were living on its banks, the Mohicans on the east, and the Minnisinks on the west side, hereditary enemies of the Iroquois, with whom they must yet have deadly doings, and sat down at the Mohawk's door. Wars with the Esopus Indians will yet cut them off at times from New Amsterdam, and often no "yachts" will pass up the river but in fear of battle, and bringing tales of treachery and massacre. That once fearful association of ideas, which was long the terror of New England houses, of "French and Indians," and the consequent midnight slaughter and conflagration, and the dreary after-tale of captivity in Canada, will draw very near to their own humble dwellings: but these few Dutch, with their poor little stockade, were putting their hands unwittingly on the key of the continent, and were about to hold some of its wildest tribes in a

leash of inviolable treaties for a century and a half,
until the mighty struggle for a continent should be
fought out around them. Who were they?

In answering, let us look only at the general
qualities of the people, such as made them fit instru-
ments in the molecular activities of that microscopic
cellule of science, from which science would now tell
us the universe primarily, and human history re-
cently, has all been evolved. As I look at them,
they were the only colonists which the proliferous
cellule aforesaid could have concatenated into such
results. If I knew the proper scientific terms, I would
pause here and indulge in a pæan to the mighty
unthinking and unreasoning Cellule. In my ignorance I must feel that praise is due to One before
whom the lakes had been always lying open, the
rivers always known from fountain to salt sea, the
races always been guided—or left unguided, if you
will—until the year of grace came for a new development of human progress,—even Him, who "ruleth in
the kingdom of men, and appointeth over it whomso-
ever He will."

The Dutch, at the beginning of the seventeenth
century, were divided into three classes—the nobles,
the citizens, and country people, or "boors." They
and their land are almost a paradox. The land—the
Nether-land, the hollow land—had been rescued from
the Northern Ocean by enormous dykes, and once at
least saved from destruction by turning the wild sea
back upon it to defeat their fiercer human foes. They
had been oppressed by the religious wrath of the

Spaniard until the totem of the Iroquois, the *tortoise*, might have been fairly claimed as their own. They were made, like the tortoise, to bear injuries and burdens which would have crushed any other organism, and which only compacted their constitutional vigor, and condensed a world of power under their thick, hard shell. The Spanish barbarities had shorn them of every grace of imagination, had injured and distressed them to the last degree of human endurance, and had failed utterly to move their phlegm or crush their torpid and dauntless resolution. Suddenly, at the first breathing-place which was granted to them, the Dutch rose to become one of the leading nations of Europe, conquerors, and successful explorers on every sea. We have not, however, to deal with that part of their history. They, too, had learned the power of union, and the advantages of righteous dealing with all men, when, as a part of a greater commercial scheme, and almost by accident, they began to colonize this country. There was one great difference between them and the other European nations which were competing for this continent. The men of Plymouth went forth as "pilgrims and strangers," under more or less of religious enthusiasm. Religion entered prominently into the professions of those who followed Lord Baltimore and William Penn. Each party sought here that "freedom to worship God," which meant, mostly, after their own fashion. The Spaniards and French were driven also by what was known to them as their religion, which implied also chivalrous national feeling. They came with the cross in one hand and the flag of their country in the other. It was not discontent with the Government at home which drove them forth, but rather an intense enthusiasm of religious patriotism.

It was quite otherwise with the Dutch. It was mainly a quiet scheme of commercial colonists, such as sends myriads of men across the Atlantic now. They had no wrongs to escape, no brilliant schemes of new lands to conquer. They came simply to secure their share of the trade which had begun to rouse the attention of the busy merchants of their country. And they were not all of one ilk in Holland. There were castes among them. The boors, who came first, formed the bulk of the population of the United Netherlands. They were the *tiers état*, whose liberties had hardly been regarded by either nobles or townsmen. These farmers were of very humble and patient character, thrifty on smallest incomes, able and willing to live hard, to amass meager gains, to look carefully after pennies or groschen, to live peaceably with all men, without fierceness, chivalry, or pride, but not without sauerkraut and beer. Contrasted with the fiery Latin races, they were insensible to the disturbances of imagination which encumbered their progress. They had no broad plains in Holland, where a party of forty knights, barbaric as Saracens, could ride down and slaughter forty thousand Jacquerie; or, had there been such, they would have been the suffering peasants and not the vain-glorious knights. They had the virtues of contented, toiling agriculturists, and such victories as were dear to them had been mostly won by the Fabian policy of patient endurance. Or, compared with the English, they were free from the fierce conscience of the Puritans, and the loose consciences of the others. It was natural that the Pilgrims, being Bible-expounders and elect saints, ✤ should pass a statute in 1633, in the Massachusetts colony, to "confirm to the Indians" the little patches of land around their wigwams, where they raised their corn and beans, and declare the rest of the land the property of the whites, on the authority of chapter i., Genesis, "and the invitation of the Indians." * And it was quite as natural that the red men, having been careless readers of Genesis, and by no means sure of their election, should demur at this private interpretation of the first chapter, and· fail to recognize it peacefully as the oracle of God. We recall here the fine scorn of Washington Irving at the claims which were set up to this continent by the right of discovery, and the proud supremacy of intelligence as against ignorance on the part of Protestants, and the rights which were given to the Catholic nations by the empty formulas of the Pope. The Dutch had neither plea to offer. They had none of that peculiar conscience which biassed all the others and brought them face to face with the untaught savages as religiously predetermined enemies. Hence, the other colonies, one by one, were involved in ceaseless wars with the natives, with intervals of hollow truce. There was an essential incapacity in the parties for peace. How the imagination turns from such dark records to fancy what might have been our

* Doc., etc., etc., Vol. XIII., p. vi.

history if all men coming hither had been Christians in heart and soul. The sad chronicles of Las Casas, and others after him, would have been more like the book of Acts, to tell of bloodless victories over willing Tlascalans and Aztecs, and others. "The dew of that birth would have been of the womb of the morning," as new nations would have learned a true Gospel of the Cross, which Cortes and Pizarro flashed in their eyes and disgraced by their deeds. The brilliant record of the courage and martyrdoms of the Jesuit missionaries to the Hurons loses something of its interest as we recall the prevailing corruption of the French nation and the infamous *Parc-aux-cerfs*, where a most Catholic king had set up a harem more revolting than that of Turk or Mormon. With all our reverence for Puritan and Quaker, one sadly dreams now over what might have been, had either of them substituted Christian practice for doctrine in their treatment of the weaker races. It is —and that alone is now my point—it is a fact of record that they all became involved in bitter wars with the natives; that they alike slowly and steadily pressed them back and exterminated them. We feel that, given the elements of the tragedy in each case, the result was bound to be the destruction of the red men. An abyss yawned between the parties, and the Indian, like Dives in the parable, called in vain across it for some Lazarus to be sent to him to alleviate the horrors of his fiery doom. I shall not denounce the one, nor dissolve in pity over the other. Suffer me to dream of what might have been, of what some day will be, when the *Christus Consolator* shall be seen to stand as the ruler of nations, the strong and weak alike:

" Folding together, with the all-tender might
Of His great love, the dark hands and the white."

The Dutch agricultural boors, who had seated themselves at Fort Orange, I will not claim for them imagination to grasp the issues which were before them, or to plan the deep foundations of a just and mighty government. I do not hold them up as models of anything sublime and far-seeing. I do not need to do so. They were *just* to the Indian. They were wonderfully patient with his ignorance and follies, and constitutionally phlegmatic to the annoyances of his vanity and braggadocio. They had no thought of his land as a deodand or a papal gift. They could not have quoted to him Genesis, chapter i., nor flaunted the oriflamme and the cross before his vision. They bought his lands and they paid for them, as per contract, taking care to make a fair bargain, and scrupulously filling the bill. They bought his furs and sold him rifles and brandy, both equally sure to kill. They made covenants with him, and they religiously observed them. The Iroquois often taunted them for stupidity, for tameness and cowardice; never for unfaithfulness or treachery. They seemed to the warriors often like the tortoise drawing in his head and observing the position of "masterly inactivity." But was not the "totem" of the tortoise well known to them? They knew that they could yet put coals of fire on his back, and the inactivity would cease. I am only interested to claim that the average Dutchman, by his patience and phlegm, by the virtues which he had learned slowly but effectually from Spanish contempt and cruelty, from his training in the flatlands of the European delta, and by his simple, unwarlike and tolerant piety, had the character which was best fitted to deal with the Iroquois, to win his esteem and hold it against tremendous odds, and transmit it to the English who came after him in 1664. They treated the Indians as men. In practice, by individual temperament, and by laws that were honestly maintained, they traded with them to their satisfaction.

By law every settler could choose his lands wherever it suited him, but he must first extinguish the Indian title.* The Dutchman was singularly tolerant in matters of religion, thanks partly to the tyranny of Spain. He did not disturb his neighbors by his zeal. He was also contented with little. I find a paper of Cornelis Van Tienhoven, Secretary of the Province, among the documents of the colony, which was sent to Holland, encouraging emigration and detailing *how* able-bodied men and women could live, and what would

* "Rule 26 of the 'Freedoms and Exemptions Granted by the West India Company to all Patrons, Masters or Private Persons who will plant colonies in New Netherlands, adopted June 7, 1629, says : " Whosoever shall settle any colony out of the limits of Manhattan Island shall be obliged to satisfy the Indians for the lands they shall settle upon." The numerous Indian deeds in this volume go to show how this rule was, as I stated above, always strictly enforced, and the tradition of the purchase of Manhattan Island proves that even at their first coming the Dutch had no intention of acquiring the land they coveted by any other means than by purchase.'" Doc., etc., etc., Vol. XIII., p. vi.

be done for them if they came.* It proves that they were able to get down to the hard-pan of economy, and lay the foundations of a great state, by living for a while in cellars hardly better than the *tepees* of the savages.

We may despise all this, but then we might have blundered contemptuously by a stable of old in Bethlehem, or disregarded the chamber in Jerusalem where a few ignorant, unlearned men were once discussing a new sort of spiritual forces. This patience and simple endurance of hardship, if it likened them outwardly to the savages, also secured their sympathy and confidence. The Dutch could point to the fact of an influence over the fierce, intractable tribes of the West, when wars were to be prevented and captives were to be redeemed, which only they could exercise. The Iroquois understood and trusted them, and them alone.

In 1614, a charter and a name were given to this province — New Netherland. In 1615, Hendrik Christiansen built a truck-house and military post on Castle Island, just below the site of Albany, with a garrison of twelve men, and called it Nassau. A few annual inundations and ice blockades drove them out of it, and in 1623, Fort Orange was built on higher ground, "just beyond the pines," with palisades reaching down to the river. Eighteen families were settled in huts of bark about the fort. Kilaen Van Rensselaer, by successive purchases from the Indians, became patroon or proprietor of the region about Fort Orange, and to secure his rights by law,

---

* Doc., etc., Vol. IV., pp. 25–36.

was required to plant there a colony of at least fifty families. In 1624, Cornelis Jansen, armed with all powers except that of inflicting capital punishment, began to govern the post. That same year a ship returned to Holland laden with valuable furs, and the colony was reported to be "bravely prosperous." Hither came the Mohawks to trade. They entered into treaty relations, which were renewed with much solemnity from time to time, and were never disturbed. There was, in fact, a time when the Dutch had no friends but the Mohawks. The Eastern colonists were contemptuously set against them. "The Dutch," said the faithful warriors of the Five Nations, "are our brethren. With them we keep but one council-fire; we are united by a covenant chain."* In 1664, the English took possession of the colony, and the Dutch rule, but not the Dutch influences, ended. As late as 1689, De Callières, Governor of Canada, speaks of Albany as being "about as large as Montreal, containing about one hundred and fifty houses and three hundred inhabitants capable of bearing arms, the majority of whom are Dutch, and some French refugees, with some English." He states that "the greater part of the inhabitants, both of Manathe (Manhattan) and Orange were then Dutch, and all Protestants, who will doubtless receive the commands of the Prince of Orange, in case England should resent the taking possession of the Hudson by France." † Again, as late as 1721, the Marquis Vandreuil speaks in his dispatches of sending messengers "to the Dutch at

* Bancroft, Vol. II., p. 66.   † Doc. Hist., Vol. I., pp. 288–291.

Orange, to remonstrate against the new settlement at Chouëguën." *

In 1665, Corlaer received a party of French and Algonquins at Schenectady, which was then returning from an expedition against the Five Nations. He was a private citizen, but was so much honored by the Indians that they always afterward called the English Governor " the Corlaer."

In 1666, another French expedition was made against the Mohawks, which succeeded only in inflaming their minds with hatred against a murderous and treacherous nation. Afterward Denonville and Frontenac also assaulted them in vain.

We must now turn to the brilliant record of the French occupation of the regions lying along the St. Lawrence and to the north of Lake Ontario, with a single remark of Colden in his history, that " the French had no hopes of persuading the Five Nations to break with New York directly," which union, he says, " always obstructed, and often defeated, the design the French had, of subjecting all North America to the crown of France." † We propose to trace briefly the development of this design. It took shape slowly, but was held with consistent pertinacity for a century. The French were always united by wise counsels, from both the political and ecclesiastical authorities at home. The English were always distracted, inconsistent, and dilatory, until, by a change of ministry, William Pitt was called for a short time to assume the management of affairs—

* Doc. Hist., Vol. I., p. 445.
† Cadwallader Colden's Hist., Part I., chap. iii., p. 43.

a time long enough, however, to annihilate the French scheme.

Champlain, after the discovery of the lake which bears his name, returned thrice to France, and, in 1615, came to Tadoussac with four Récollet (Franciscan) priests. He went with a party of Algonquins by the head-waters of the Ottawa, and discovered Lake Huron. On his return he reached Lake Ontario, and passed along its eastern shores. The Franciscans began at once their labors as missionaries, but were soon displaced by the Jesuits, who, under the name of " the black robes," were afterward known as the mighty " medicine men " of the whites. Their story has the charm of a romance. The sturdiest Protestant must pause to wipe away the tear that gathers, as he reads of their heroism in penetrating pathless wilds; their humility in accepting all manner of insults and hardships from sensual, brutal savages; their zeal in continuing the offices of religion in leafy huts or under the shade of trees, often with wine pressed from the wild grapes by their own hands, and sometimes transubstantiated into the blood of martyrs; their ceaseless catechisings of children and adults, whose minds were clouded by ages of ignorance and inhumanity; their disregard of all the attractions of society; their " deaths oft " with or for their catechumens, sometimes surrendering themselves to tortures that they might confess a penitent or baptize a candidate with drops of dew gathered from the ears of maize contemptuously thrown to them for food. Nero's blazing candles and Spain's Inquisition in the Low Countries were simple contrivances compared with the tortures of the cannibal tribes into whose hands they fell. But nothing daunted or delayed them. As one fell, another, at the command of his superior, took up his crucifix and entered a Huron canoe, and went away into the wilderness, trusting, as Père Mesnard said, "to the Providence that feeds the birds and clothes the wild flowers of the forest." Nobles of France lived and died in this work, for the conversion of the Hurons —no less, or little less, for the glory of France.*

To conquer souls for Jesus, to extend the honor of their order, and to open new lands for the standard of the lilies, was motive, incentive, and reward enough for men who saw in it the certain beatitudes of piety on earth and beyond it. It is a strange, — I fancy it is an unparalleled, record. Condemn their faults, their superstition, their treachery as politicians, as we may, he must be hard indeed who does not feel a tremor of his highest sensibilities at the name of Râle defying the New England bullets on the Kennebec, to save his flock ; or Père Jogues, meekly submitting to appalling anguish at the hands of the Iroquois ; or Mesnard, reasoning that if the latter could reach the Chippewas for murder, he too

* We have a specimen of the ordinary motives of the missionaries, in the person of Father Claude Alloüez (1665). "He arrived on the first day of October, at a great council of ten or twelve nations, at the great village of the Chippewas, in the Bay of Chegoimegon." "In the name of Louis XIV., and his viceroy, he commanded peace, and offered commerce and an alliance against the Iroquois ; the soldiers of France would smooth the path between the Chippewas and Quebec ; would brush the pirate canoes from the river ; would leave the Five Nations no choice between tranquillity and destruction." Bancroft, Vol. III., p. 150.

must venture thither for the Gospel's sake. It is very strange that these Jesuits made no marked impression on the Iroquois. They seemed to all other tribes as men of another world. The American savage always looks upon the insane and maniacal as inspired, and reverences them as beings in communion with superior powers of good and evil. The enthusiasm of the Jesuits exalted them to the borders of such inspiration. They claimed to work miracles, to wash out sins forever, to bring out of the wafer and wine-cup the mysterious *sang réal*, to anoint with the mystic unction of peace the dying warrior, and speed him to the land of the Great Spirit, and they dared and died to prove ·their zeal. They seldom failed. They failed effectually to move the Five Nations. The few converts given to them among that people they were compelled to gather around the Island of Montreal, thenceforth exiles, lost to their former friends.

With the Jesuit went forth the fur-trader and trapper. Launching their batteaux on the chill waters of the Ottawa, these voyageurs toiled through grim wildernesses, now at the oar, now at the dangerous rapids, and anon over the muddy, tangled portages, pushing on and on westward to Huron, to the straits of Mackinaw and the Sault St. Mary, and setting their traps far up on the streams that turn north toward Hudson's Bay. He, too, had a native fitness for the work before him—a religious conscience that availed him, and a patriotic fire that could feed his fancy, where the wild animals of the chase, or the wilder savages, who often chased him, were his only neighbors. He had the skill to cook all manner of creatures of or under the earth, and could hobnob with the aborigines over their raw meat and pounded corn, and ignore their dirt and vulgarity. He had, too, the religion of the Parc-aux-cerfs of his most Christian Majesty at Paris, and could find a savage wife in every tribe, and mate his constancy to her canine chastity. He could carry his vanity and braggadocio uninjured everywhere, and wrap himself in it and defy the savagery of nature and the ridicule of savages. He cared nothing for the rights of man or of colonial charters. The English had nothing of this; more, they were vexing themselves about political questions and colonial rights. The corrupt court of the Hanoverian princes was petrified in selfishness and petty tyranny, all the while that the subtle Frenchmen were pushing on their advance and laying the foundations of a mighty empire. The English hardly saw what was before their eyes. "The English," said the French officers to Colonel Washington at Venango, "can raise two men to our one, but they are too dilatory to prevent any enterprise of ours.* The enterprise which was just then in their minds was the closing the possession of the tract lying between the Ohio River and Lake Erie.

These, then, were the armies which France sent · out as the *avant-couriers* of discovery. "Not a cape was turned," says the historian, "nor a river entered, but a Jesuit led the way." The voyageur followed fast, and a great trade sprang up on the St. Law-

---

* Bancroft's Hist., Vol. III., p. 71.

rence, which incited and rewarded his daring indus-
try. Strangely enough again, the Dutch could and
did always undersell them, and thus again checked
their advance into the regions of the Five Nations.

In 1634, the Jesuits Brebeuf and Daniel, and
soon after "the gentle Lalemant," established the
first house of the Society of Jesus on the shores of a
bay of Lake Huron. The French were shut off from
Lake Ontario, and their line of advance to this mis-
sionary trading-post was by the Ottawa, over per-
haps "fifty cataracts and five and thirty portages."

We pass on now to mention certain names which
bear upon my proposition.

In 1673, forty years after this first mission-house
was built, Père Marquette and the layman Joliet and
five other Frenchmen, with two Algonquins as guides,
carrying their canoes on their shoulders, set out on
the 10th of June to cross the short space of less than
two miles which separates the Fox River from the
Wisconsin, thus leaving the streams which run toward
Quebec. With a prayer to the Immaculate Virgin,
they embarked on the latter, and in seven days were
floating on the waters of the Mississippi. They en-
dured many dangers and hardships in their long journey down the stream, past the mouth of the Arkansas,
to a region where snows were unusual, and satisfy-
ing themselves that the great river ran into the Gulf,
and not into the Pacific or the Atlantic, they returned
to Canada and reported the unfinished discovery.
"The fame" of this report of Joliet, says Bancroft,
"fired the ambition of Colbert." I am inclined to

insert the name of Talon, the Intendant of Canada, between Joliet and Colbert, as being the first to grasp the advantages of the discovery.*

About this time Robert de la Salle had obtained a grant of land at Fort Frontenac, in Canada, where the city of Kingston now stands, with a "right to trade with the Five Nations." His imagination became excited by the news brought by Joliet, and by the older tales of Columbus and De Soto, and he sighed for nobler worlds to conquer. He, too, would dare the perilous journey and add new glories to French conquest. Returning to France, he found out Colbert, that greatest of financial statesmen, and communicated his plans to him and his son Seigneley. They entered with zeal into them. He was given all that he asked, and was commissioned to carry out the scheme. He was directed to complete the discovery of the river, to establish a fort at the mouth of it, as a defense against the Spanish, "and to secure the communication of Canada with the West Indies." This plan finally included a chain of forts and strong trading-posts across the country between the St. Lawrence and the Mississippi, in order to hold possession of it and secure his advance.

This was in 1678. The next year La Salle built and launched the first vessel that ever sailed upon Lake Erie—the "Griffon," a boat of sixty tons. He planted a colony at Niagara, established a trading-post at Michilimackinac, passed through Lake Michigan, and anchored in Green Bay. ·Sending back thence the "Griffon" with a load of furs, he started in

* Bancroft, Vol. II., p. 332.

canoes for the head of Lake Michigan, and built there a small fort among the Miamis. Then, December 3d, he passed on with Father Hennepin and Tonti to Kankakee. Sailing down the river, he reached an Illinois village and made another fort, which, in the bitterness of his soul, he named "Crèvecœur," the "fort of the broken heart," near the present city of Peoria. Leaving Tonti in command, he returned on foot, with three companions, to Canada for supplies. He learned there the loss of the "Griffon," and also of a ship which had been sent over with supplies. Making up another party, he started again for fort Crèvecœur, where he found that the Iroquois had attacked Tonti, who had retreated to Green Bay. He went down the Illinois River to its mouth, and again returned to Canada to gather his companions and obtain fresh resources. At last, in 1681, this man of iron will overcame all obstacles and succeeded in traversing the Mississippi downward to its mouth. He explored three of its channels, and on April 9th, 1682, he set up a column with the French arms upon it, and took formal possession of the territory. Returning to Quebec, he went again to France. There he received a patent, to his wish, of boundless grants along the river. Colbert had died, but Seigneley, his son, who succeeded, seconded his applications, and Louis XIV. gave him letters authorizing him to discover the western parts of New France, and to build forts, bestowing on him "the seigniory of the government of the forts which he should erect on his route." La Salle "proposed to the king to unite Canada with Louisiana, and extend his sovereignty to the Gulf, and received from him instructions to return and immediately to colonize Louisiana." He fitted out a naval expedition for the mouth of the river, which ended in shipwreck·and ruin to him, and, while seeking his way back to Canada, he was murdered by his companions. He perished miserably, but the results of his discovery remained.

About the year 1699, Iberville built a fort upon the banks of the river, and in 1718, New Orleans was commenced. From that period we must leave to your imagination the uninterrupted advance of the French power. They possessed the friendship of almost all the tribes along the great circle which stretches from Quebec around the lakes and down the Great River to its mouth. Nearest to them, to the south and east, were the Spaniards in Mexico and Florida and the West Indies. The English were confined to the Atlantic coast, shut in by the natural barrier of the long ridges of mountains, which begin with the spurs of the Adirondacks and sink down into the uplands of Alabama and Georgia. The French nation was at one with their colonies — the English never at one with theirs. The strongest religious bonds united the former. Jesuit missions dotted the rivers and lakes with an obedient army of men ready to become martyrs for their church or for France. No question of rights, no vexatious duties or stamp acts, interfered with the home commerce. It was a commerce of mutual benefit. The central power of the throne demanded and received the same obedience at the far-off trading-post, among savage tribes, which it received in the outskirts of

Paris. Those historians are correct who, like Froude, find a paramount cause of the success of the Reformation in England in the weariness of discord which followed the Wars of the Roses. So, the unified, compact, unquestioned power of the Bourbons can be traced back to a similar weariness of the strifes of rebellious nobles and religious factions. Patriotism and religion in the French breast had come to mean absolute rule in Church and State, and unmurmuring, heroic óbedience from every citizen. We have, then, the opposing conditions of the great struggle of the eighteenth century for the mastership of this continent. The odds were all with the French — were all against the English. Here and there, for a little while, the latter awoke to the fact that the French were absorbing all the trade with the Indians, were creeping steadily along the lakes and drawing supplies from lands hardly known to them by name, on the north and west of them, and were advancing up the Great River and its streams that sprang from the Alleghanies, and were impressing on the natives the sense of the power and ubiquity of the Grand Monarque. Colden, who wrote in 1647, told the English in London that " Indian affairs in Canada were the care of the Government,—in New York, of traders,"—and hence came the wise policy of the one and the folly shown by the others!

Another influence from home came to the aid of the French scheme. You remember that this colony was the próvince of the Duke of York, afterward King James the Second. The one wish of the Canadians was to send the Jesuit priests among the Five

Nations; the policy of the New York "traders" was
by all means to keep them out. There was reason
enough for their distrust. The Jesuits were politicians as well as religionists. What so natural for them
as to bring these intractable savages to the knowledge
of the cross and obedience to the lilies. Of course,
the Duke of York sent orders that Jesuit priests must
be received among the Iroquois. The governors and
people were helpless. The priests are said to have
incited parties of the Five Nations to make war on
friendly Indians in Virginia and Maryland, hoping
thus to disturb the peace, and compel the English to
punish them and drive them into the arms only too
willing to receive them. They failed. The Governor
of Maryland sent Colonel Coursey, in 1677, to meet
the tribes at Albany and renew their friendship. The
treaty was reinforced, and the prisoners that had been
taken were mostly returned. The tribes who were
absent from the meeting sent in their adherence, and
the plan fell through.

Let me here put together a few dates.

In 1646, fourteen years from the restoration of
Quebec, France had her posts on the Kennebec and
on Lake Huron, and had approached the settlement
at Albany by a fort commanding Lake Champlain.

In 1689, forty years afterward, Chevalier De Cal-
·lières developed his plan to capture Fort Orange and
Manhattan Island, in order to become master of the
Iroquois, "and thus establish their (the French) race."
He confesses that the Dutch were able to trade with
the Indians and give them bargains, "nearly a half less
·than his Frenchmen could afford, and were likely to

destroy the trade in peltries,"* then sustaining Canada and largely benefiting the mother country. His plan was approved, and Sieur De Frontenac was under orders to carry it out; but it came to nothing beyond burning Schenectady and the massacre of its inhabitants. In 1685, the Marquis Denonville invaded the Genesee country, and, as Colden words it, "got nothing but dry blows by this expedition." In 1696, Frontenac entered the Mohawk country with a thousand French and two thousand Indians. He surprised a castle at Oneida, and destroyed some standing corn. The English looked on tamely, though one Colonel Fletcher reports "that a rumor of *his* approach caused them to beat a retreat." Half a century later, in 1743, the wily policy of the French has stolen on toward its object. Governor Clarke writes of " the vast increase of the French trade since the peace of Utrecht; of their steady advance to link together the Mississippi and Lake Ontario; of two forts at Frontenac and Niagara; of two vessels of fifty or sixty tons on that lake, by the mastery of which they acquire power over the Indians; of their intrigues with the Five Nations, whose old chiefs still remain faithful and restrain the younger men; of their certain result in separating the Five Nations and destroying them in detail, having already cowed their spirit." Meanwhile, they had fastened themselves on Lake Champlain to control the Mohawks, and the English were only idly looking on, to see the great circle joined which would shut them off finally from the trade which was then so valuable.

* Documentary History of N. Y., Vol. I., p. 286.

, Therefore, in 1757, with many victories and much successful policy to warrant it, the French proudly "claimed and seemed to possess twenty parts in twenty-five of this continent, leaving four only to Spain and but one to Great Britain." Abroad, England had hardly done better. To all human calculation, the struggle was about to end in favor of France.

Fort Duquesne, at the junction of the Mononga-hela and Alleghany rivers, was one pole of her great battery; the fort at Erie, on the lake, was the other. Two or three stockades on the space between were uniting the poles, and the circle would be complete, and New France would soon rival the old in power. The one bar to success had always been the treaty faith between the Iroquois and the Corlaer.*

But the struggle was about to end in the defeat of the French, and I have kept you too long to do it justice. Fortunately for my purpose, you are all sufficiently familiar with the two closing scenes of the great drama. It is only necessary for me to link them to the third fact occurring across the ocean, and my work is done.

The French had been everywhere successful. When Montcalm roused the echoes of Ganouski Bay on Lake George, on the morning of that summer day,

* "During a century of contention with France, the friendship of the Five Nations, in possession of the great mountain barrier between Canada and the upper Hudson, turned the scale and counterbalanced the great advantages which lay on the side of France. But for this the whole course of our history might have been changed; New York might now belong to France, and the other States might still be colonies of England." Doc, Hist. N. Y., Vol. I., p. vi.

4

August 2, 1757, as he started to assault Fort William Henry, at the head of the lake, fifteen hundred savages of thirty-three tribes, collected from the shore of the Kennebec in the east, to Sandusky Bay in the west, from the Montaignais and St. Francis tribes along the river and the Hurons of the North, raised their war-whoop in answer to his reveille. The Frenchman was free of the woods. The Englishman crept through them in fear, and fled back to his towns with thanksgiving. The narrative of Lake George and of Braddock's defeat alike show the skill and united purpose of the French, the stupid disorder and timid confusion of the English. General Webb lay inactive at Fort Edward, in sound of the cannon battering down Fort William Henry, and dared not stir to help it. The dash, the courage, the successes, were all on the wrong side. The French were masters. They and their dusky allies had learned to despise the ignoble Anglais, and the Iroquois wondered at their inaction and lack of courage. We read the sad story with feelings of shame at its unvarying disgrace. Colonists, busy with their separate interests, meanly confounded all generalship, and the home government slumbered on until a continent had almost slipped from their grasp.

Thus it came to pass that one of the events of the final drama began without plan or honor. Where Pittsburg now stands was a wilderness claimed by the English, as given to them by a treaty with the Iroquois; and a hunter, one Gist, was called from the Upper Yadkin, and sent to explore the lands beyond the Monongahela. An effort followed to build a small fort at its junction with the Alleghany, in 1754. It was a far-off land, and known only to a few hunters like Gist. The French claimed the land by right of possession, and simply wiped out the stockade and scattered its occupants. They in turn built a fort, which Captain Contrecœur called after the Governor of Canada, Duquesne, and meant it, as he said, to become "the great center of the French in all that country." Then came General Braddock upon the scene, as proud as Walpole and as inefficient, to lead his eight thousand men—the largest force that had ever been raised in the colonies—to a disgraceful panic and massacre. We here get a glimpse of the young Virginian surveyor as he tries to teach the unteachable general, and then is busy in saving the remnant of the beaten host. It was a foolish, shameful campaign ; but, read backward, and it was all of a piece with the administration of the colonies for years before.

It was found that the treaty of Utrecht * had omitted to determine the lines of demarcation between the races, especially as to the Iroquois question, and hence came the old French war.

It helped the downfall of the corrupt English ministry, and George II., despite his hostility to him, was

* The treaty of Utrecht (1713) determined that "France should never molest the Five Nations subject to the dominion of Great Britain." The French claimed, according to a recognized figment of state policy of that age, by discovery and some spots of possession, all lands bordering on the lakes, and, therefore, of the lands on which the Five Nations were found. The treaty shut them off from molesting the people who lived on their land. This anomaly the treaty of Aix la Chapelle (1748) failed to appreciate and remove. The French pushed into their lands. The English appealed in behalf of the people under their dominion, and a resort to arms was the result.

compelled by public opinion to summon William Pitt to the head of affairs in 1757. Called to power by the will of the people, and only for the few closing years of an inglorious reign, he nobly fulfilled their expectations. His energetic and wise measures were felt to the remotest point of the empire. The tide of success turned. The men sent to capture Fort Ticonderoga knew that the Premier, as our boys say, "meant business." Amherst led his army across Lake George to victory, and the French were forced to evacuate Crown Point and leave the lake free to the English. Fully awake to the importance of the blows about to be struck, the English minister determined to cut the great circle that had been so long forming at the points on the Ohio and on the St. Lawrence. Bradstreet captured Fort Frontenac, on Ontario, and gained the command of the lakes. In 1758, Major Grant made an ineffectual assault on Fort Duquesne, and General Forbes, urged on by Colonel Washington, with six thousand men sat down before it, when, November 25, the French set fire to it, and retreated down the river by its light.

The next year Admiral Saunders conveyed General Wolfe and an army of eight thousand men from Louisburg to besiege Quebec. On June 27th they landed on Orleans Island, and began operations by a useless bombardment of the city. Montcalm looked down on him from the citadel and easily outgeneraled him. The short summer slipped away and the foe was inaccessible, and likely to remain so. Then came to him one of those inspirations which are something more than accidents. Ten years before no Englishman would have dared the venture that Wolfe made. Pitt was behind him, and the prize was a continent.

On the evening of September 12th, Wolfe, wrapped in a boat-cloak, was busy on the river scrutinizing the cliffs to find a path to the summit. It was remembered afterward, that, as the boat was silently drifting under the cliffs in the autumn twilight, Wolfe was busy in dreamland, and full of the tenderness of a poem of his loved England. He was heard to repeat the lines of Gray's "Elegy":

> " The boast of heraldry, the pomp of power,
> And all that beauty, all that wealth e'er gave,
> Await alike the inevitable hour —
> The paths of glory lead but to the grave."

He turned to his companion and said: "I had rather be the author of those lines, than be the victor in to-morrow's battle."

The next day, as Wolfe stood on the Heights of Abraham with his army, the dreamy mood had passed from him. He was the actor, then, in one of the most important scenes of our country's history, and filled the part with honor. The struggle of a century culminated where the path of glory had led him up those steeps to an early grave; but it was also the grave of the dream of Latin power on this side of the Atlantic. Dying, he heard the distant shout of the soldiers: "They run! they run!"—and died happy. The next day died also Montcalm — the splendid cavalier, the polished marquis, the chivalrous nobleman, whose name comes to us adorned with many virtues, but also incarnadined by the massacre of Lake George, which neither the limpid waters there, nor " all great Neptune's ocean " can wash " clean " again. On the 18th, Quebec surrendered, and four years afterward Canada was ceded to Great Britain.

The French scheme had failed. The perpetual barrier to its success for a hundred and fifty years, which no religious zeal, nor diplomacy, nor greed, nor threats, nor actual wars could ever abate or remove, was the friendship of the Iroquois for the Dutch. There is no parallel to it in the colonial records. We suspect that there could not have been one. The men who followed Miles Standish would have treated the Mohawks as they did the Pequods. The Virginians were not exemplary for patience, justice, or forbearance. The Quakers did make an effort after fair treatment, but their virtues were antagonisms to the natives.

If I have fairly sketched the parties and the facts, I now leave you to judge whether I said too much, when I claimed that there was a manifest Providence in the fact that the Dutch rather than the English first came into possession of the valleys of the Hudson and the Mohawk, and thus into connection with the Iroquois, gained their lasting friendship and bound them in an iron chain of treaty-faith for a century and a half, till the dying Wolfe heard the shout of victory on the Plains of Abraham.*

* The same year France lost India by the victories of Clive, and her navy by the victories of Hawke and others, and came out of the war humiliated and crippled, with her finances exhausted and her commerce destroyed. Her religion fared little better. The miserable king was soon compelled to banish the Jesuits, and the golden age of in-

And if this be true, must we not honor the virtue of the patient, honest, and industrious race who, not ignorant of evils, learned to pity the miserable and to deal fairly and humanely with them? While we give a thought of compassionate regret for the splendid athletes who have mostly passed away from the hunting-grounds of their fathers, which were for that period the key of the position, we may leave them with the Judge of all the Earth, and thank God for the rich heritage which the Corlears of the past secured for us and for our children, from their friendship.

fidelity blossomed out, in such men as Voltaire, Rousseau, Diderot, and others, and in works like the great " Dictionnaire Encyclopédique."

www.ingramcontent.com/pod-product-compliance
Lightning Source LLC
Chambersburg PA
CBHW031758090426
42739CB00008B/1068